Survey of College Plans for MOOCs

ISBN: 978-1-57440-260-5
Library of Congress Control Number: 2013952016
© 2013 Primary Research Group, Inc.

TABLE OF CONTENTS

LIST OF TABLES

THE QUESTIONNAIRE

COLLEGE DEVELOPED MOOCS

1. Does your college itself offer MOOCs, or does it participate in a partnership or consortia that offer MOOCs from your college?

2. If your college does offer MOOCs, either directly or through another party, how many courses does it offer?

3. If your college offers its own MOOCs or plans to develop them, what subject areas are you initially focusing on?

4. If your college offers its own MOOCs or plans to develop them, what is your overall developmental budget for this effort?

5. Approximately how many individuals, faculty, administrators, and staffers would you say are involved in creating MOOCs at your institution?

6. How high a priority is it for your institution to develop your own massive open online courses (MOOCs)?

    A. Very high priority
    B. High priority
    C. A priority
    D. Not a priority
    E. Not considering it

7. How likely do you think it will be for your institution to develop and offer a MOOC within the next three years?

    A. Already offer them
    B. Highly likely
    C. Likely
    D. Unlikely
    E. Definitely not

8. If your college or any of its academic or administrative departments has established a task force in an effort o develop MOOCs or to find ways to use taped classroom lectures in other ways, please describe this effort or series of efforts.

9. Does your institution distribute videos or tapes of classroom lectures at your college on _____?

    A. Vimeo
    B. YouTube

C.   Facebook
D.   Google

LECTURE CAPTURE

10. Does your college employ lecture capture or course taping technology through which it tapes courses for students or faculty to view later?

11. If your college does employ lecture capture/course taping technology, approximately how many courses do you now have on tape?

12. If you have these tapes, what are you doing with them or what do you plan to do with them?

13. Does the college maintain a centralized repository or archive of any kind for its taped lectures, MOOCs, or other intellectual property based on lectures or classes given by the college's faculty?

14. Which academic or administrative departments are the biggest users of MOOCs or taped lectures?

AWARDING CREDIT FOR MOOCS

15. **Has your college accepted credits for any MOOCs taken previously by students entering the college or by current students of the college?**

16. Explain the likely evolution of your college's policies in this area. Is it likely to accept credit from MOOCs in the near future? With what provisos or conditions? Does the college have a task force or group looking into these issues?

17. Has your college face pressure to adopt MOOCs and/or to offer courses for credit from MOOCs at your institution?

18. Does your college have an agreement with _____ to offer MOOCs to your students for credit?

     A.   Coursera
     B.   Udacity
     C.   EdX
     D.   Udemy
     E.   Khan Academy

19. Has your college had discussions with or sought preliminary information from _____ as a possible prelude to using any of their resources?

     A.   Coursera

B. Udacity
C. EdX
D. Udemy
E. Khan Academy

20. If your college is using MOOCs from another college or from an established provider, or is planning to do so, in what subject areas are you most likely to introduce MOOCs?

OPINION OF MOOCS

21. Which phrase best approximates your attitude toward MOOCs?

   A. Destructive and not as effective as education
   B. More or less a fad unlikely to have lasting impact
   C. A useful new technology likely to have a significant impact when improved
   D. A useful technology that is having a significant impact right now
   E. A significant advance that will lower costs and improve educational quality

22. To what extent do you believe that instruction via MOOCs needs to be supplemented by tutors or other kinds of instructors?

23. Do you believe that MOOCs, either as presently constructed or as rewired in a blended learning setting, constitute an advance in education effectiveness and/or cost control?

COPYRIGHT AND MOOCS

24. What measures has the college taken to assure copyright protection for the institution's MOOCs or for taped lectures, classes, or special events sponsored by the college?

25. Some MOOCs are from for-profit companies and therefore the fair use provisions of copyright law offer less protection to end users who use copyright materials in their online courses. Has your college taken special measures to assure that instructors in blended learning classes that employ MOOCs do not violate copyright? If so, what are these measures?

SURVEY PARTICIPANTS

Abilene Christian University
American International College
Buena Vista University
Buffalo State College
Claremont McKenna College
Coe College
Colgate University
College of Education at James Madison University
Crown College of the Bible
Duke University
Eastern New Mexico University – Roswell
Fielding Graduate University
Gogebic Community College
Graceland University
Harrisburg University
International Baptist College and Seminary
Iowa State University
John Carroll University
Lindsey Wilson College
McKendree University
Medaille College
Mercer County Community College
Mississippi Community College Board
Mountain Empire Community College
Muhlenberg College
New College Oxford
Nicholls State University
Ocean County College
Ramapo College of New Jersey
Rend Lake College
Salish Kootenai College
Shanghai University of Finance & Economics
Sheridan College
Southern Vermont College
St. Catharine College
St. Francis Xavier University
Texas Christian University
Texas State Technical College
Texas Tech University
Union University
University of Arkansas
University of Bergen
University of Central Lancashire

University of Hawaii – West Oahu
University of Missouri-Kansas City
University of North Carolina at Greensboro
University of North Texas Health Science Center
University of Pittsburgh at Bradford
University of Rochester
University of South Dakota
University of St. Thomas
Warren Wilson College
Wayne State University
Winona State University

CHARACTERISTICS OF THE SAMPLE

Overall sample size: 56

By Public or Private Status
Public	30
Private	26

By Annual Full-Time Tuition
Less than $5,000	14
$5,000 to $14,999	17
$15,000 to $24,999	13
$25,000 or more	12

By Type of College
Community college	9
4-year college	25
MA/PhD-granting college	9
Research university	13

By Full-Time Student Enrollment
Less than 2,500	19
2,500 to 7,499	20
7,500 or more	17

SUMMARY OF MAIN FINDINGS

Who are the Producers of MOOCs?

Only a little more than 7 percent of the colleges sampled currently offer any kind of MOOC or contribute as a partner to an academic consortia or coalition that produces MOOCs. All MOOC producers in our sample were private colleges and about two-thirds were research universities. Some 4-year colleges also said that they were currently producing MOOCs either alone or in partnership with other colleges.

Number of Courses Offered by MOOC Producers

The number of courses offered by those colleges producing MOOCs ranged dramatically from 2 to 250. Mean and median information, 67.5 and 9, respectively, is useful insomuch as it suggests that two kinds of colleges are producing MOOCs: the major producers, offering hundreds of courses, and a range of other colleges that are putting their toes in this new "market" or "development" and producing a few MOOCs to evaluate the experience. We expect a great deal more of this in the coming few years, with colleges producing a few MOOCs in niche areas, getting experience, and assessing the results.

Spending on MOOC Production

Only five colleges gave data on how much they are spending to develop MOOCs. One said it is spending a million dollars, while others are spending between $1,000 and $8,500 per course. Once again, a few colleges are making serious efforts and most others are just dipping their toes in the market, keeping their costs down. The number of individuals involved in the MOOC development effort ranges from 2 to 30, with many including about 10 individuals in the MOOC task force.

Likelihood of MOOC Production by Type of College

We asked the survey participants how high a priority it was for them to develop MOOCs. We gave them five possible answers: 1) Very high priority, 2) High priority, 3) A priority, 4) Not a priority, and 5) Not considering it. The most common answer was "not a priority" and close to 64 percent gave this answer, and another 20 percent said flatly that they were "not considering it." 9.1 percent, however, considered the development of MOOCs "a priority" and 3.64 percent considered it a "high priority" while the same percentage considered it "very high priority." About 11.5 percent of the private colleges in the sample considered MOOC development to be a "high priority" or "very high priority" while only 3.45 percent of public colleges fell into one of these two categories. On the other hand, more than 17 percent of public colleges considered it "a priority" while no private colleges did, all of which suggests that the public colleges, at least at present, are just beginning to dip in this market while the private colleges are much closer to actual development.

To try to pin down the actual likely behavior of colleges regarding MOOC development, we asked the survey participants flatly how likely was it for their college to offer a MOOC (even a single MOOC) within the next three years. We gave them five possible answers: 1) Already offer them (5.45 percent), 2) Highly likely (10.91 percent), 3) Likely (30.91 percent), 4) Unlikely (42.7 percent), and 5) Definitely not (5.45 percent). One of the most interesting results was the very high percentage of community colleges in the sample that feel that they will be offering MOOCs within the next three years, as more than 22 percent thought it highly likely and 44.4 percent thought it likely that they would be offering MOOCs within the next three years.

Use of Lecture Capture Technology: Prelude to MOOCs?

The college effort to develop MOOCs often grows out of pre-existing efforts to use lecture capture technology to tape and preserve classroom lectures as a form of intellectual property. Many colleges now tape their lectures and we wanted to examine how they use and distribute these tapes, hoping that this may provide some insight into their ultimate plans for MOOCs.

Distribution of Taped Class Lectures via Internet Channels

One motivation for taping lectures is to use them as promotional tools by showing classes on the internet, particularly through major video sites such as Vimeo or YouTube. 5.36 percent of the colleges surveyed distribute videos of their classes through Vimeo. All of those that do so are public colleges, most of which are community colleges, particularly larger ones, with low annual tuition. More than 30 percent of the colleges sampled distribute classroom lectures on YouTube. This time the data is more evenly split between public and private colleges and the former are only somewhat more likely to distribute classroom lectures in this way. Nonetheless, there is a strong negative correlation between tuition levels and the tendency to distribute classroom lectures on YouTube. Indeed, the higher the tuition, the less likely is a college to distribute their lectures over YouTube, perhaps suggesting that the long term populism of MOOCs will run into very definite limits. 50 percent of the colleges in the sample with tuitions of less than $5,000 per year distribute some of their classroom lectures over YouTube while only 16.67 percent of colleges charging more than $25,000 per year for tuition do the same.

Only 7.14 percent distribute taped lectures over Facebook. Interestingly, and perhaps oddly, all are private colleges, mostly in the higher tuition ranges, and all of which are 4-year colleges with enrollments of fewer than 2,500 students. No college outside of this description distributes video of classroom lectures over Facebook. Only 3.57 percent distribute video of classroom lectures over Google. Once again, all are private colleges in the higher tuition ranges and all are 4-year colleges with enrollments of less than 2,500 students.

Overall 54.55 percent of the colleges in the sample employ lecture capture including 69 percent of public colleges and nearly 77 percent of the research universities. The mean number of courses captured on tape was 55.24 with a range of 1 to 292 and a median of 20. For the most part, these lectures are currently being used as back-up material by the lecturers in the courses themselves as a resource for their students who missed a class or who want to review a class. Some are also using them in distance learning programs.

We wanted to know how much further processing these tapes received after the initial taping. 37 percent of the colleges sampled have developed some kind of centralized repository or archive for their taped lectures. More than 53 percent of research universities have done so. We asked which departments were the largest users of the taped lectures and perhaps the only clear trend was that nursing programs, and allied health programs in general, tended to be heavier users than others.

Percentage of Colleges That Award Academic Credit for MOOCs

7.84 percent of the colleges sampled have awarded credit for MOOCs. Most were private colleges and none were community colleges. Many colleges are looking into the issue of accepting MOOC credit and are actively seeking ways to measure the knowledge gained through MOOCs. The responses suggest that a minority of colleges might be looking to accept MOOC credit in the near future if some kind of reassuring mechanism could be devised to assess knowledge gained through MOOCs and if the colleges feel sufficient pressure from state governments, accreditation bodies, and even the general student public.

Percentage of Colleges That Say They Have Been Pressured to Accept MOOC Credit

Close to 8 percent of colleges sampled say that they have felt pressure to adopt MOOCs and/or to accept credit for courses from MOOCs of other institutions. Interestingly, private colleges were slightly more likely than public colleges in the sample to have felt this pressure.

Colleges That Have Reached Agreements with Major MOOC Producers

We asked the colleges in the sample if they have any agreements with any of the major MOOC services to offer MOOCs for credit at their institution. First we asked about Coursera, and just 1.79 percent of institutions sampled have such an agreement with Coursera. None have an agreement with Udacity, nor do any with EdX. Similarly, no colleges in the sample have an agreement with Udemy, though 1.79 percent have an agreement with Khan Academy.

Percentage of Colleges That Have Approached MOOC Producers for Information or Preliminary Talks

While only 1.79 percent of the colleges sampled had an actual for-credit agreement with Coursera, 10.71 percent had held discussions or sought preliminary information from Coursera as a prelude to using any of their resources. Nearly 15.4 percent of the private colleges in the sample have had such contacts with Coursera.

A smaller number, 5.6 percent, have approached Udacity for preliminary talks or information about the use of the service. All of the interest in Udacity was from private, 4-year colleges. 3.57 percent had approached EdX, once again all private colleges. The same percentage have approached Khan Academy though interest here was mostly from community colleges. None had approached Udemy for preliminary information.

College Administrator Opinion of MOOCs

We asked the colleges in the sample their opinion of MOOCs. We asked them to choose one of five possible alternative evaluations: 1) Destructive and not effective as education, 2) More or less a fad unlikely to have lasting impact, 3) A useful new technology likely to have a significant impact when improved, 4) A useful technology that is having a significant impact right now, and 5) A significant advance that will lower costs and improve educational quality. Only 1.96 percent thought of MOOCs as destructive while 19.61 percent thought them more or less a fad. However, the majority (nearly 57 percent) believed them to be a useful new technology likely to have a significant impact when improved. Another 13.73 percent believed that they were a useful technology that is having a significant impact right now and another 7.84 percent through that they were a significant advance and that they will lover the costs and improve the quality of higher education.

Perceived Need to Supplement MOOCs with Other Forms of Instruction

We asked whether instruction via MOOCs needs to be supplemented by other kinds of instruction. Comments varied but most believed that such supplementation was essential and some were actively working on plans to do so.

1. College Developed MOOCs

Table 1.1: Does your college itself offer MOOCs, or does it participate in a partnership or consortia that offers MOOCs from your college?

	Yes	No
Entire sample	7.14%	92.86%

Table 1.2: Does your college itself offer MOOCs, or does it participate in a partnership or consortia that offers MOOCs from your college? Broken out by public or private status of the college.

Public or Private	Yes	No
Public	0.00%	100.00%
Private	15.38%	84.62%

Table 1.3: Does your college itself offer MOOCs, or does it participate in a partnership or consortia that offers MOOCs from your college? Broken out by annual full-time tuition.

Tuition	Yes	No
Less than $5,000	7.14%	92.86%
$5,000 to $14,999	5.88%	94.12%
$15,000 to $24,999	0.00%	100.00%
$25,000 or more	16.67%	83.33%

Table 1.4: Does your college itself offer MOOCs, or does it participate in a partnership or consortia that offers MOOCs from your college? Broken out by type of college.

Type of College	Yes	No
Community college	0.00%	100.00%
4-year college	8.00%	92.00%
MA/PhD-granting college	0.00%	100.00%
Research university	15.38%	84.62%

Table 1.5: Does your college itself offer MOOCs, or does it participate in a partnership or consortia that offers MOOCs from your college? Broken out by the college's full-time student enrollment for all programs and schools.

Enrollment	Yes	No
Less than 2,500	5.26%	94.74%
2,500 to 7,499	10.00%	90.00%
7,500 or more	5.88%	94.12%

Table 1.6: If your college does offer MOOCs, either directly or through another party, how many courses does it offer?

	Mean	Median	Minimum	Maximum
Entire sample	67.50	9.00	2.00	250.00

Table 1.7: If your college does offer MOOCs, either directly or through another party, how many courses does it offer? Broken out by public or private status of the college.

Public or Private	Mean	Median	Minimum	Maximum
Public	N/A	N/A	N/A	N/A
Private	67.50	9.00	2.00	250.00

Table 1.8: If your college does offer MOOCs, either directly or through another party, how many courses does it offer? Broken out by annual full-time tuition.

Tuition	Mean	Median	Minimum	Maximum
Less than $5,000	250.00	250.00	250.00	250.00
$5,000 to $14,999	2.00	2.00	2.00	2.00
$15,000 to $24,999	N/A	N/A	N/A	N/A
$25,000 or more	9.00	9.00	3.00	15.00

Table 1.9: If your college does offer MOOCs, either directly or through another party, how many courses does it offer? Broken out by type of college.

Type of College	Mean	Median	Minimum	Maximum
Community college	N/A	N/A	N/A	N/A
4-year college	126.00	126.00	2.00	250.00
MA/PhD-granting college	N/A	N/A	N/A	N/A
Research university	9.00	9.00	3.00	15.00

Table 1.10: If your college does offer MOOCs, either directly or through another party, how many courses does it offer? Broken out by the college's full-time student enrollment for all programs and schools.

Enrollment	Mean	Median	Minimum	Maximum
Less than 2,500	250.00	250.00	250.00	250.00
2,500 to 7,499	67.25	8.50	2.00	250.00
7,500 or more	3.00	3.00	3.00	3.00

If your college offers its own MOOCs or plans to develop them, what subject areas are you initially focusing on?

1. Bible and Theology.

2. Finance, Economics, Accounting.

3. Plans to develop MOOC in Math.

4. Broad range.

5. Moral Thought.

6. Health care with emphasis on education for the new workforce related to the Affordable Care Act.

7. Public Health, Basic Sciences.

8. Science, Humanities, Psychology, Native Studies.

9. Music.

10. The college administration would like to offer MOOCs in all areas.

11. Interactive Media.

12. Two MOOCs being developed.

13. We would like to develop a MOOC for Developmental Mathematics.

If your college has developed or is developing MOOCs, what is your overall developmental budget for this effort?

1. $1,000 per course per instructor. Development stipend.

2. $1 million.

3. $5,000.

4. Faculty course release and instructional designer regular load.

5. $8,500 plus personnel time.

Approximately how many individuals, faculty, administrators, and staffers would you say are involved in creating MOOCs at your institution?

1. At least 30.

2. 10.

3. Maybe 1 or 2.

4. About 10.

5. 12.

6. 8.

7. 10.

8. 2.

9. 2.

10. 3.

Table 1.11: How high a priority is it for your institution to develop your own massive open online courses (MOOCs)?

	Very high priority	High priority	A priority	Not a priority	Not considering it
Entire sample	3.64%	3.64%	9.09%	63.64%	20.00%

Table 1.12: How high a priority is it for your institution to develop your own massive open online courses (MOOCs)? Broken out by public or private status of the college.

Public or Private	Very high priority	High priority	A priority	Not a priority	Not considering it
Public	3.45%	0.00%	17.24%	58.62%	20.69%
Private	3.85%	7.69%	0.00%	69.23%	19.23%

Table 1.13: How high a priority is it for your institution to develop your own massive open online courses (MOOCs)? Broken out by annual full-time tuition.

Tuition	Very high priority	High priority	A priority	Not a priority	Not considering it
Less than $5,000	7.69%	0.00%	15.38%	53.85%	23.08%
$5,000 to $14,999	5.88%	5.88%	17.65%	52.94%	17.65%
$15,000 to $24,999	0.00%	0.00%	0.00%	76.92%	23.08%
$25,000 or more	0.00%	8.33%	0.00%	75.00%	16.67%

Table 1.14: How high a priority is it for your institution to develop your own massive open online courses (MOOCs)? Broken out by type of college.

Type of College	Very high priority	High priority	A priority	Not a priority	Not considering it
Community college	0.00%	0.00%	11.11%	55.56%	33.33%
4-year college	8.00%	4.00%	4.00%	64.00%	20.00%
MA/PhD-granting college	0.00%	0.00%	0.00%	75.00%	25.00%
Research university	0.00%	7.69%	23.08%	61.54%	7.69%

Table 1.15: How high a priority is it for your institution to develop your own massive open online courses (MOOCs)? Broken out by the college's full-time student enrollment for all programs and schools.

Enrollment	Very high priority	High priority	A priority	Not a priority	Not considering it
Less than 2,500	5.26%	0.00%	0.00%	68.42%	26.32%
2,500 to 7,499	0.00%	10.00%	10.00%	50.00%	30.00%
7,500 or more	6.25%	0.00%	18.75%	75.00%	0.00%

Table 1.16: How likely do you think it will be for your institution to develop and offer a MOOC within the next three years?

	Already offer them	Highly likely	Likely	Unlikely	Definitely not
Entire sample	5.45%	10.91%	30.91%	47.27%	5.45%

Table 1.17: How likely do you think it will be for your institution to develop and offer a MOOC within the next three years? Broken out by public or private status of the college.

Public or Private	Already offer them	Highly likely	Likely	Unlikely	Definitely not
Public	0.00%	20.00%	43.33%	30.00%	6.67%
Private	12.00%	0.00%	16.00%	68.00%	4.00%

Table 1.18: How likely do you think it will be for your institution to develop and offer a MOOC within the next three years? Broken out by annual full-time tuition.

Tuition	Already offer them	Highly likely	Likely	Unlikely	Definitely not
Less than $5,000	7.14%	28.57%	42.86%	14.29%	7.14%
$5,000 to $14,999	5.88%	11.76%	35.29%	41.18%	5.88%
$15,000 to $24,999	0.00%	0.00%	25.00%	75.00%	0.00%
$25,000 or more	8.33%	0.00%	16.67%	66.67%	8.33%

Table 1.19: How likely do you think it will be for your institution to develop and offer a MOOC within the next three years? Broken out by type of college.

Type of College	Already offer them	Highly likely	Likely	Unlikely	Definitely not
Community college	0.00%	22.22%	44.44%	22.22%	11.11%
4-year college	8.33%	4.17%	12.50%	66.67%	8.33%
MA/PhD-granting college	0.00%	11.11%	44.44%	44.44%	0.00%
Research university	7.69%	15.38%	46.15%	30.77%	0.00%

Table 1.20: How likely do you think it will be for your institution to develop and offer a MOOC within the next three years? Broken out by the college's full-time student enrollment for all programs and schools.

Enrollment	Already offer them	Highly likely	Likely	Unlikely	Definitely not
Less than 2,500	5.56%	0.00%	16.67%	72.22%	5.56%
2,500 to 7,499	10.00%	5.00%	30.00%	45.00%	10.00%
7,500 or more	0.00%	29.41%	47.06%	23.53%	0.00%

If your college or any of its academic or administrative departments has established a task force in an effort to develop MOOCs or to find ways to use taped classroom lectures in other ways, please describe this effort or series of efforts.

1. We have a distance Doctoral program, but they come in periodically for face-to-face lectures.

2. Center for teaching and learning working with one specific department.

3. Converting Town and Gown initiatives into MOOC format.

4. Flipped classroom.

5. Not planning to develop MOOCs, but beginning to discuss ways to make recordings of educational events/courses available to currently enrolled students.

6. No formal effort is underway at this time.

7. We established an Advisory Committee of faculty at the college and university levels and created an Associate Vice Provost for Online and Digital Educational Initiatives.

8. Actively working to pilot a series of "Flipped Classroom" courses. Reviewing option to embed the MOOC of another (larger name university) as a "module" within an institutionally offered course. I would be the instructor and my intent would be to oversee student progress using the MOOC for supplementary content.

9. Task force on online and distance education will report to Faculty Senate and Senior Leadership team for approval.

10. The Division of Continual Learning has set a MOOC Task Force.

11. We have been incorporating digital video lectures into existing online courses.

12. Provide the link of the MOOCs on the guides of the corresponding subjects on the LibGuides platform of the library.

13. Ongoing project for communicating classroom lectures on video.

14. Working on courses that would feed into academic programs.

15. Lecture capture is in very early stage of investigation. Plans are to develop targeted pilot projects intended to identify adoption factors.

16. We are using video lectures as in Khan Academy.

Table 1.21:   Does your institution distribute videos or tapes of classroom lectures at your college on Vimeo?

	Yes	No
Entire sample	5.36%	94.64%

Table 1.22:   Does your institution distribute videos or tapes of classroom lectures at your college on Vimeo? Broken out by public or private status of the college.

Public or Private	Yes	No
Public	10.00%	90.00%
Private	0.00%	100.00%

Table 1.23:   Does your institution distribute videos or tapes of classroom lectures at your college on Vimeo? Broken out by annual full-time tuition.

Tuition	Yes	No
Less than $5,000	14.29%	85.71%
$5,000 to $14,999	5.88%	94.12%
$15,000 to $24,999	0.00%	100.00%
$25,000 or more	0.00%	100.00%

Table 1.24:   Does your institution distribute videos or tapes of classroom lectures at your college on Vimeo? Broken out by type of college.

Type of College	Yes	No
Community college	22.22%	77.78%
4-year college	0.00%	100.00%
MA/PhD-granting college	0.00%	100.00%
Research university	7.69%	92.31%

Table 1.25:   Does your institution distribute videos or tapes of classroom lectures at your college on Vimeo? Broken out by the college's full-time student enrollment for all programs and schools.

Enrollment	Yes	No
Less than 2,500	0.00%	100.00%
2,500 to 7,499	5.00%	95.00%
7,500 or more	11.76%	88.24%

Table 1.26: Does your institution distribute videos or tapes of classroom lectures at your college on YouTube?

	Yes	No
Entire sample	30.36%	69.64%

Table 1.27: Does your institution distribute videos or tapes of classroom lectures at your college on YouTube? Broken out by public or private status of the college.

Public or Private	Yes	No
Public	33.33%	66.67%
Private	26.92%	73.08%

Table 1.28: Does your institution distribute videos or tapes of classroom lectures at your college on YouTube? Broken out by annual full-time tuition.

Tuition	Yes	No
Less than $5,000	50.00%	50.00%
$5,000 to $14,999	23.53%	76.47%
$15,000 to $24,999	30.77%	69.23%
$25,000 or more	16.67%	83.33%

Table 1.29: Does your institution distribute videos or tapes of classroom lectures at your college on YouTube? Broken out by type of college.

Type of College	Yes	No
Community college	55.56%	44.44%
4-year college	36.00%	64.00%
MA/PhD-granting college	22.22%	77.78%
Research university	7.69%	92.31%

Table 1.30: Does your institution distribute videos or tapes of classroom lectures at your college on YouTube? Broken out by the college's full-time student enrollment for all programs and schools.

Enrollment	Yes	No
Less than 2,500	26.32%	73.68%
2,500 to 7,499	35.00%	65.00%
7,500 or more	29.41%	70.59%

Table 1.31: Does your institution distribute videos or tapes of classroom lectures at your college on Facebook?

	Yes	No
Entire sample	7.14%	92.86%

Table 1.32: Does your institution distribute videos or tapes of classroom lectures at your college on Facebook? Broken out by public or private status of the college.

Public or Private	Yes	No
Public	0.00%	100.00%
Private	15.38%	84.62%

Table 1.33: Does your institution distribute videos or tapes of classroom lectures at your college on Facebook? Broken out by annual full-time tuition.

Tuition	Yes	No
Less than $5,000	7.14%	92.86%
$5,000 to $14,999	0.00%	100.00%
$15,000 to $24,999	15.38%	84.62%
$25,000 or more	8.33%	91.67%

Table 1.34: Does your institution distribute videos or tapes of classroom lectures at your college on Facebook? Broken out by type of college.

Type of College	Yes	No
Community college	0.00%	100.00%
4-year college	16.00%	84.00%
MA/PhD-granting college	0.00%	100.00%
Research university	0.00%	100.00%

Table 1.35: Does your institution distribute videos or tapes of classroom lectures at your college on Facebook? Broken out by the college's full-time student enrollment for all programs and schools.

Enrollment	Yes	No
Less than 2,500	21.05%	78.95%
2,500 to 7,499	0.00%	100.00%
7,500 or more	0.00%	100.00%

Table 1.36: Does your institution distribute videos or tapes of classroom lectures at your college on Google?

	Yes	No
Entire sample	3.57%	96.43%

Table 1.37: Does your institution distribute videos or tapes of classroom lectures at your college on Google? Broken out by public or private status of the college.

Public or Private	Yes	No
Public	0.00%	100.00%
Private	7.69%	92.31%

Table 1.38: Does your institution distribute videos or tapes of classroom lectures at your college on Google? Broken out by annual full-time tuition.

Tuition	Yes	No
Less than $5,000	0.00%	100.00%
$5,000 to $14,999	0.00%	100.00%
$15,000 to $24,999	7.69%	92.31%
$25,000 or more	8.33%	91.67%

Table 1.39: Does your institution distribute videos or tapes of classroom lectures at your college on Google? Broken out by type of college.

Type of College	Yes	No
Community college	0.00%	100.00%
4-year college	8.00%	92.00%
MA/PhD-granting college	0.00%	100.00%
Research university	0.00%	100.00%

Table 1.40: Does your institution distribute videos or tapes of classroom lectures at your college on Google? Broken out by the college's full-time student enrollment for all programs and schools.

Enrollment	Yes	No
Less than 2,500	10.53%	89.47%
2,500 to 7,499	0.00%	100.00%
7,500 or more	0.00%	100.00%

2. Lecture Capture

Table 2.1: Does your college employ lecture capture or course taping technology through which it tapes courses for students or faculty to view later?

	Yes	No
Entire sample	54.55%	45.45%

Table 2.2: Does your college employ lecture capture or course taping technology through which it tapes courses for students or faculty to view later? Broken out by public or private status of the college.

Public or Private	Yes	No
Public	68.97%	31.03%
Private	38.46%	61.54%

Table 2.3: Does your college employ lecture capture or course taping technology through which it tapes courses for students or faculty to view later? Broken out by annual full-time tuition.

Tuition	Yes	No
Less than $5,000	53.85%	46.15%
$5,000 to $14,999	76.47%	23.53%
$15,000 to $24,999	38.46%	61.54%
$25,000 or more	41.67%	58.33%

Table 2.4: Does your college employ lecture capture or course taping technology through which it tapes courses for students or faculty to view later? Broken out by type of college.

Type of College	Yes	No
Community college	37.50%	62.50%
4-year college	52.00%	48.00%
MA/PhD-granting college	44.44%	55.56%
Research university	76.92%	23.08%

Table 2.5: Does your college employ lecture capture or course taping technology through which it tapes courses for students or faculty to view later? Broken out by the college's full-time student enrollment for all programs and schools.

Enrollment	Yes	No
Less than 2,500	36.84%	63.16%
2,500 to 7,499	57.89%	42.11%
7,500 or more	70.59%	29.41%

Table 2.6: If your college does employ lecture capture/course taping technology, approximately how many courses do you now have on tape?[*]

	Mean	Median	Minimum	Maximum
Entire sample	55.24	20.00	1.00	292.00

Table 2.7: If your college does employ lecture capture/course taping technology, approximately how many courses do you now have on tape? Broken out by public or private status of the college.

Public or Private	Mean	Median	Minimum	Maximum
Public	54.39	17.50	1.00	292.00
Private	57.43	25.00	2.00	150.00

Table 2.8: If your college does employ lecture capture/course taping technology, approximately how many courses do you now have on tape? Broken out by annual full-time tuition.

Tuition	Mean	Median	Minimum	Maximum
Less than $5,000	20.00	5.00	1.00	50.00
$5,000 to $14,999	77.36	20.00	2.00	292.00
$15,000 to $24,999	43.00	20.00	5.00	90.00
$25,000 or more	87.50	87.50	25.00	150.00

Table 2.9: If your college does employ lecture capture/course taping technology, approximately how many courses do you now have on tape? Broken out by type of college.

Type of College	Mean	Median	Minimum	Maximum
Community college	26.67	25.00	5.00	50.00
4-year college	49.00	20.00	2.00	150.00
MA/PhD-granting college	31.33	5.00	4.00	85.00
Research university	83.50	32.50	1.00	292.00

Table 2.10: If your college does employ lecture capture/course taping technology, approximately how many courses do you now have on tape? Broken out by the college's full-time student enrollment for all programs and schools.

Enrollment	Mean	Median	Minimum	Maximum
Less than 2,500	61.00	85.00	2.00	110.00
2,500 to 7,499	36.57	20.00	2.00	150.00
7,500 or more	63.45	15.00	1.00	292.00

---

[*] Count the same course taught by a different instructor as an individual course. So for example, "Introduction to the History of Spain" taught by Jones and "Introduction to the History of Spain" taught by Smith would count as two courses.

If you have these tapes, what are you doing with them or what do you plan to do with them?

1. Allow men and women with competing priorities to use them to finish their programs.

2. Just use the videos for reviewing the lecture. Only one course uses the taped lecture for online delivery.

3. Make it as the open educational resources o once the permission is given from the copyright owners.

4. These are used for repetition of the course during the next cycle of instruction, particularly in the EMS program and the new Community Paramedic program.

5. Used for the individual courses and then reviewed and revamped for the next course.

6. These digital files are deleted after the term as they are deemed the intellectual property of the lecturer. Therefore, they are only utilized for the specific term within which they were recorded.

7. Archive them in the library until they rot.

8. Nothing beyond making them available to students in that particular class.

9. Use them when courses are repeated as support materials.

10. Use for online education.

11. Offering them to our students taking online courses through the LMS.

12. I personally use it for those who didn't make it to the lecture.

13. Archive them.

14. No plans.

15. Lecturers control usage.

16. Nothing.

17. Used for on-demand viewing in Blackboard by students during a course, and later archived for future use.

18. Not sure beyond making them available to our students.

19. Use them as a resource for students.

20. Making them available to the University's constituency.

21. The tapes are for the benefit of the students enrolled in the courses for review and study. The disciplines that use lecture-capture tend to be high content, high stakes testing disciplines (e.g., nursing) and programs that offer course on intensive formats.

22. Further develop course in Moodle for use in a classroom or for online instruction.

Table 2.11: Does the college maintain a centralized repository or archive of any kind for its taped lectures, MOOCs, or other intellectual property based on lectures or classes given by the college's faculty?

	Yes	No
Entire sample	37.04%	62.96%

Table 2.12: Does the college maintain a centralized repository or archive of any kind for its taped lectures, MOOCs, or other intellectual property based on lectures or classes given by the college's faculty? Broken out by public or private status of the college.

Public or Private	Yes	No
Public	37.93%	62.07%
Private	36.00%	64.00%

Table 2.13: Does the college maintain a centralized repository or archive of any kind for its taped lectures, MOOCs, or other intellectual property based on lectures or classes given by the college's faculty? Broken out by annual full-time tuition.

Tuition	Yes	No
Less than $5,000	30.77%	69.23%
$5,000 to $14,999	47.06%	52.94%
$15,000 to $24,999	41.67%	58.33%
$25,000 or more	25.00%	75.00%

Table 2.14: Does the college maintain a centralized repository or archive of any kind for its taped lectures, MOOCs, or other intellectual property based on lectures or classes given by the college's faculty? Broken out by type of college.

Type of College	Yes	No
Community college	12.50%	87.50%
4-year college	37.50%	62.50%
MA/PhD-granting college	33.33%	66.67%
Research university	53.85%	46.15%

Table 2.15: Does the college maintain a centralized repository or archive of any kind for its taped lectures, MOOCs, or other intellectual property based on lectures or classes given by the college's faculty? Broken out by the college's full-time student enrollment for all programs and schools.

Enrollment	Yes	No
Less than 2,500	22.22%	77.78%
2,500 to 7,499	42.11%	57.89%
7,500 or more	47.06%	52.94%

Which academic or administrative departments are the biggest users of MOOCs or taped lectures?

1. Faculty of law.

2. Bible and Theology.

3. Diverse population.

4. Library.

5. Division of Health.

6. Agriculture.

7. Medical School.

8. Sciences.

9. College of Arts and Sciences.

10. Business.

11. Our adult degree-completion program.

12. Chemistry, Medicine, Biology, Pharmacy.

13. Foundations.

14. Math.

15. Business, Nursing.

16. Economics and Finance.

17. Social Sciences.

18. Office of Strategic Initiatives.

19. Nursing; School of Professional Counseling.

20. Ministry.

21. Social Sciences.

22. Health Sciences: Nursing, Pharmacy, Dentistry.

How have your college's MOOCs, or the distribution of lectures from the college through YouTube, Vimeo, the college website, or other venues, affected the reputation of the college? Has the college benefited from the distribution of these resources?

1. No significant data.

2. No, not yet.

3. We believe it adds positively to the university's reputation, but we have no evidence to support that decision.

4. Thus far we see no effects.

5. Students have appreciated the flexibility.

6. Their access is tightly controlled and not advertised. I would assume our currently enrolled students benefit from these resources, but the college as a whole may not yet.

7. I do not believe our utilization of ITunes University or other modes of distribution have had any notable effect on the institution.

8. Yes – benefited.

9. Yes.

10. We have benefited.

11. Unknown.

12. We don't distribute them except to enrolled students so the reputational effect is modest to nil.

13. Not sure.

14. Not sure.

15. The College has not distributed them beyond the students enrolled in the classes that are being taped. If there has been any influence, it has been positive through presentations at conferences on how to support student learning in challenging fields.

16. No.

17. No.

18. Yes.

19. No, No.

20. Yes.

21. No.

22. Yes.

3. Awarding Credit for MOOCs

Table 3.1: Has your college accepted credits for any MOOCs taken previously by students entering the college or by current students of the college?

	Yes	No
Entire sample	7.84%	92.16%

Table 3.2: Has your college accepted credits for any MOOCs taken previously by students entering the college or by current students of the college? Broken out by public or private status of the college.

Public or Private	Yes	No
Public	3.70%	96.30%
Private	12.50%	87.50%

Table 3.3: Has your college accepted credits for any MOOCs taken previously by students entering the college or by current students of the college? Broken out by annual full-time tuition.

Tuition	Yes	No
Less than $5,000	8.33%	91.67%
$5,000 to $14,999	6.67%	93.33%
$15,000 to $24,999	7.69%	92.31%
$25,000 or more	9.09%	90.91%

Table 3.4: Has your college accepted credits for any MOOCs taken previously by students entering the college or by current students of the college? Broken out by type of college.

Type of College	Yes	No
Community college	0.00%	100.00%
4-year college	8.33%	91.67%
MA/PhD-granting college	14.29%	85.71%
Research university	8.33%	91.67%

Table 3.5: Has your college accepted credits for any MOOCs taken previously by students entering the college or by current students of the college? Broken out by the college's full-time student enrollment for all programs and schools.

Enrollment	Yes	No
Less than 2,500	10.53%	89.47%
2,500 to 7,499	5.56%	94.44%
7,500 or more	7.14%	92.86%

Explain the likely evolution of your college's policies in this area. Is it likely to accept credit from MOOCs in the near future? With what provisos or conditions? Does the college have a task force or group looking into these issues?

1. We are working on this issue, but we do not have a group yet.

2. Not yet.

3. Just beginning conversations in this area.

4. Yes. Via ACE at least.

5. Not considering it at this time.

6. We are actively discussing the options but are not to the policy/practice development stage.

7. Yes – with some documentation that identifies the credit earned by the specific individual in question.

8. Unpredictable.

9. Not likely to accept. Has no task force or group.

10. Possible. Will need a capstone test/project to verify knowledge/skill. No task force.

11. Too early to tell, and no clear direction on this.

12. As far as I know, we are only testing water to figure out some of the issues. Our student body is unlikely to present problems in large scale in the near future.

13. No.

14. Not in the near future, but if there is a reliable assessment/documentation method we will reconsider. We do not have a specific group looking into this issue except insofar as it is part of our strategic planning process.

15. May accept through ACE.

16. With our assessment.

17. Unlikely to accept.

18. Accredited proof of participation (assignments, grades).

19. I doubt we will accept MOOC credit anytime soon.

20. It would need to be credit-based and accredited.

21. Not likely to accept credit for courses without associated small group live instruction.

22. We are exploring all possible developments.

23. No task force. There have been some meetings. Reaction is in general negative from the faculty. There's interest, I think, among trustees.

24. We would follow the same procedures and policies for accepting credit as we do for transfer/transient credit from other accredited institutions.

25. As of now, the notion is that a student would be required to document their work (via a portfolio, for example) within the MOOC before being granted transfer credit. Another option is for the student to be given the opportunity to "test out" of the material in order to receive credit.

26. It is necessary to create a Task Force to study this issue.

27. To be accepted for credit, a MOOC must include evidence-based assessments.

28. No.

29. Under discussion.

30. Not likely to accept credit for MOOCs.

31. We are looking into this question.

32. It is likely that we will accept credit from MOOCs through our credit-by-experience process. Students would have to take a final exam for the course (the same final that on-campus students take) to assess their learning from the MOOC.

33. Task Force.

34. Yes, we are considering accepting credit for MOOCs that have ACE recommendations.

35. We are looking at online in general. MOOCs are really a bad idea and destroys the value of an education.

36. Yes, will accept credit.

37. Our PLA process is under examination.

38. No.

39. Yes, will accept credit in the future if student completes additional course requirements.

40. Yes, had a faculty group establish policies.

41. We would only accept credit if the student demonstrated competency on a recognized test (e.g. CLEP or other standardized measure). As an institution, we favor competency-based credit.

Table 3.6: Has your college faced pressure to adopt MOOCs and/or to offer courses for credit from MOOCs at your institution?

	Yes	No
Entire sample	7.84%	92.16%

Table 3.7: Has your college faced pressure to adopt MOOCs and/or to offer courses for credit from MOOCs at your institution? Broken out by public or private status of the college.

Public or Private	Yes	No
Public	7.41%	92.59%
Private	8.33%	91.67%

Table 3.8: Has your college faced pressure to adopt MOOCs and/or to offer courses for credit from MOOCs at your institution? Broken out by annual full-time tuition.

Tuition	Yes	No
Less than $5,000	0.00%	100.00%
$5,000 to $14,999	13.33%	86.67%
$15,000 to $24,999	15.38%	84.62%
$25,000 or more	0.00%	100.00%

Table 3.9: Has your college faced pressure to adopt MOOCs and/or to offer courses for credit from MOOCs at your institution? Broken out by type of college.

Type of College	Yes	No
Community college	0.00%	100.00%
4-year college	13.04%	86.96%
MA/PhD-granting college	0.00%	100.00%
Research university	8.33%	91.67%

Table 3.10: Has your college faced pressure to adopt MOOCs and/or to offer courses for credit from MOOCs at your institution? Broken out by the college's full-time student enrollment for all programs and schools.

Enrollment	Yes	No
Less than 2,500	11.11%	88.89%
2,500 to 7,499	0.00%	100.00%
7,500 or more	13.33%	86.67%

Table 3.11:   Does your college have an agreement with Coursera to offer MOOCs
to your students for credit?

	Yes	No
Entire sample	1.79%	98.21%

Table 3.12:   Does your college have an agreement with Coursera to offer MOOCs
to your students for credit? Broken out by public or private status of the college.

Public or Private	Yes	No
Public	0.00%	100.00%
Private	3.85%	96.15%

Table 3.13:   Does your college have an agreement with Coursera to offer MOOCs
to your students for credit? Broken out by annual full-time tuition.

Tuition	Yes	No
Less than $5,000	0.00%	100.00%
$5,000 to $14,999	0.00%	100.00%
$15,000 to $24,999	0.00%	100.00%
$25,000 or more	8.33%	91.67%

Table 3.14:   Does your college have an agreement with Coursera to offer MOOCs
to your students for credit? Broken out by type of college.

Type of College	Yes	No
Community college	0.00%	100.00%
4-year college	0.00%	100.00%
MA/PhD-granting college	0.00%	100.00%
Research university	7.69%	92.31%

Table 3.15:   Does your college have an agreement with Coursera to offer MOOCs
to your students for credit? Broken out by the college's full-time student enrollment
for all programs and schools.

Enrollment	Yes	No
Less than 2,500	0.00%	100.00%
2,500 to 7,499	5.00%	95.00%
7,500 or more	0.00%	100.00%

Table 3.16: **Does your college have an agreement with Udacity to offer MOOCs to your students for credit?**

	Yes	No
Entire sample	0.00%	100.00%

Table 3.17: **Does your college have an agreement with EdX to offer MOOCs to your students for credit?**

	Yes	No
Entire sample	0.00%	100.00%

Table 3.18: **Does your college have an agreement with Udemy to offer MOOCs to your students for credit?**

	Yes	No
Entire sample	0.00%	100.00%

Table 3.19:   Does your college have an agreement with Khan Academy to offer MOOCs to your students for credit?

	Yes	No
Entire sample	1.79%	98.21%

Table 3.20:   Does your college have an agreement with Khan Academy to offer MOOCs to your students for credit? Broken out by public or private status of the college.

Public or Private	Yes	No
Public	3.33%	96.67%
Private	0.00%	100.00%

Table 3.21:   Does your college have an agreement with Khan Academy to offer MOOCs to your students for credit? Broken out by annual full-time tuition.

Tuition	Yes	No
Less than $5,000	7.14%	92.86%
$5,000 to $14,999	0.00%	100.00%
$15,000 to $24,999	0.00%	100.00%
$25,000 or more	0.00%	100.00%

Table 3.22:   Does your college have an agreement with Khan Academy to offer MOOCs to your students for credit? Broken out by type of college.

Type of College	Yes	No
Community college	11.11%	88.89%
4-year college	0.00%	100.00%
MA/PhD-granting college	0.00%	100.00%
Research university	0.00%	100.00%

Table 3.23:   Does your college have an agreement with Khan Academy to offer MOOCs to your students for credit? Broken out by the college's full-time student enrollment for all programs and schools.

Enrollment	Yes	No
Less than 2,500	0.00%	100.00%
2,500 to 7,499	5.00%	95.00%
7,500 or more	0.00%	100.00%

Table 3.24. Has your college had discussions with or sought preliminary information from Coursera as a possible prelude to using any of their resources?

	Yes	No
Entire sample	10.71%	89.29%

Table 3.25: Has your college had discussions with or sought preliminary information from Coursera as a possible prelude to using any of their resources? Broken out by public or private status of the college.

Public or Private	Yes	No
Public	6.67%	93.33%
Private	15.38%	84.62%

Table 3.26: Has your college had discussions with or sought preliminary information from Coursera as a possible prelude to using any of their resources? Broken out by annual full-time tuition.

Tuition	Yes	No
Less than $5,000	7.14%	92.86%
$5,000 to $14,999	11.76%	88.24%
$15,000 to $24,999	15.38%	84.62%
$25,000 or more	8.33%	91.67%

Table 3.27: Has your college had discussions with or sought preliminary information from Coursera as a possible prelude to using any of their resources? Broken out by type of college.

Type of College	Yes	No
Community college	0.00%	100.00%
4-year college	16.00%	84.00%
MA/PhD-granting college	0.00%	100.00%
Research university	15.38%	84.62%

Table 3.28: Has your college had discussions with or sought preliminary information from Coursera as a possible prelude to using any of their resources? Broken out by the college's full-time student enrollment for all programs and schools.

Enrollment	Yes	No
Less than 2,500	15.79%	84.21%
2,500 to 7,499	10.00%	90.00%
7,500 or more	5.88%	94.12%

Table 3.29:   Has your college had discussions with or sought preliminary information from Udacity as a possible prelude to using any of their resources?

	Yes	No
Entire sample	5.36%	94.64%

Table 3.30:   Has your college had discussions with or sought preliminary information from Udacity as a possible prelude to using any of their resources? Broken out by public or private status of the college.

Public or Private	Yes	No
Public	0.00%	100.00%
Private	11.54%	88.46%

Table 3.31:   Has your college had discussions with or sought preliminary information from Udacity as a possible prelude to using any of their resources? Broken out by annual full-time tuition.

Tuition	Yes	No
Less than $5,000	0.00%	100.00%
$5,000 to $14,999	5.88%	94.12%
$15,000 to $24,999	15.38%	84.62%
$25,000 or more	0.00%	100.00%

Table 3.32:   Has your college had discussions with or sought preliminary information from Udacity as a possible prelude to using any of their resources? Broken out by type of college.

Type of College	Yes	No
Community college	0.00%	100.00%
4-year college	12.00%	88.00%
MA/PhD-granting college	0.00%	100.00%
Research university	0.00%	100.00%

Table 3.33:   Has your college had discussions with or sought preliminary information from Udacity as a possible prelude to using any of their resources? Broken out by the college's full-time student enrollment for all programs and schools.

Enrollment	Yes	No
Less than 2,500	10.53%	89.47%
2,500 to 7,499	5.00%	95.00%
7,500 or more	0.00%	100.00%

Table 3.34:   Has your college had discussions with or sought preliminary information from EdX as a possible prelude to using any of their resources?

	Yes	No
Entire sample	3.57%	96.43%

Table 3.35:   Has your college had discussions with or sought preliminary information from EdX as a possible prelude to using any of their resources? Broken out by public or private status of the college.

Public or Private	Yes	No
Public	0.00%	100.00%
Private	7.69%	92.31%

Table 3.36:   Has your college had discussions with or sought preliminary information from EdX as a possible prelude to using any of their resources? Broken out by annual full-time tuition.

Tuition	Yes	No
Less than $5,000	0.00%	100.00%
$5,000 to $14,999	5.88%	94.12%
$15,000 to $24,999	0.00%	100.00%
$25,000 or more	8.33%	91.67%

Table 3.37:   Has your college had discussions with or sought preliminary information from EdX as a possible prelude to using any of their resources? Broken out by type of college.

Type of College	Yes	No
Community college	0.00%	100.00%
4-year college	4.00%	96.00%
MA/PhD-granting college	0.00%	100.00%
Research university	7.69%	92.31%

Table 3.38:   Has your college had discussions with or sought preliminary information from EdX as a possible prelude to using any of their resources? Broken out by the college's full-time student enrollment for all programs and schools.

Enrollment	Yes	No
Less than 2,500	0.00%	100.00%
2,500 to 7,499	10.00%	90.00%
7,500 or more	0.00%	100.00%

Table 3.39:   Has your college had discussions with or sought preliminary information from Khan Academy as a possible prelude to using any of their resources?

	Yes	No
Entire sample	3.57%	96.43%

Table 3.40:   Has your college had discussions with or sought preliminary information from Khan Academy as a possible prelude to using any of their resources? Broken out by public or private status of the college.

Public or Private	Yes	No
Public	3.33%	96.67%
Private	3.85%	96.15%

Table 3.41:   Has your college had discussions with or sought preliminary information from Khan Academy as a possible prelude to using any of their resources? Broken out by annual full-time tuition.

Tuition	Yes	No
Less than $5,000	7.14%	92.86%
$5,000 to $14,999	5.88%	94.12%
$15,000 to $24,999	0.00%	100.00%
$25,000 or more	0.00%	100.00%

Table 3.42:   Has your college had discussions with or sought preliminary information from Khan Academy as a possible prelude to using any of their resources? Broken out by type of college.

Type of College	Yes	No
Community college	11.11%	88.89%
4-year college	4.00%	96.00%
MA/PhD-granting college	0.00%	100.00%
Research university	0.00%	100.00%

Table 3.43:   Has your college had discussions with or sought preliminary information from Khan Academy as a possible prelude to using any of their resources? Broken out by the college's full-time student enrollment for all programs and schools.

Enrollment	Yes	No
Less than 2,500	5.26%	94.74%
2,500 to 7,499	5.00%	95.00%
7,500 or more	0.00%	100.00%

Table 3.44: Has your college had discussions with or sought preliminary information from Udemy as a possible prelude to using any of their resources?

	Yes	No
Entire sample	0.00%	100.00%

If your college is using MOOCs from another college or from an established provider, or is planning to do so, in what subject areas are you most likely to introduce MOOCs?

1. General education

2. Management, Business

3. Media Psychology

4. Economics, Business

5. Mission Seminars

6. Business

7. General Education

4. Opinion of MOOCs

Table 4.1: Which phrase best approximates your attitude toward MOOCs?

	Destructive and not effective as education	More or less a fad unlikely to have lasting impact	A useful new technology likely to have a significant impact when improved	A useful technology that is having a significant impact right now	A significant advance that will lower costs and improve educational quality
Entire sample	1.96%	19.61%	56.86%	13.73%	7.84%

Table 4.2: Which phrase best approximates your attitude toward MOOCs? Broken out by public or private status of the college.

Public or Private	Destructive and not effective as education	More or less a fad unlikely to have lasting impact	A useful new technology likely to have a significant impact when improved	A useful technology that is having a significant impact right now	A significant advance that will lower costs and improve educational quality
Public	3.70%	22.22%	55.56%	11.11%	7.41%
Private	0.00%	16.67%	58.33%	16.67%	8.33%

Table 4.3: Which phrase best approximates your attitude toward MOOCs? Broken out by annual full-time tuition.

Tuition	Destructive and not effective as education	More or less a fad unlikely to have lasting impact	A useful new technology likely to have a significant impact when improved	A useful technology that is having a significant impact right now	A significant advance that will lower costs and improve educational quality
Less than $5,000	0.00%	7.69%	69.23%	15.38%	7.69%
$5,000 to $14,999	6.67%	20.00%	46.67%	20.00%	6.67%
$15,000 to $24,999	0.00%	30.77%	46.15%	7.69%	15.38%
$25,000 or more	0.00%	20.00%	70.00%	10.00%	0.00%

Table 4.4: Which phrase best approximates your attitude toward MOOCs? Broken out by type of college.

Type of College	Destructive and not effective as education	More or less a fad unlikely to have lasting impact	A useful new technology likely to have a significant impact when improved	A useful technology that is having a significant impact right now	A significant advance that will lower costs and improve educational quality
Community college	0.00%	12.50%	62.50%	12.50%	12.50%
4-year college	4.35%	26.09%	52.17%	13.04%	4.35%
MA/PhD-granting college	0.00%	0.00%	75.00%	12.50%	12.50%
Research university	0.00%	25.00%	50.00%	16.67%	8.33%

Table 4.5: Which phrase best approximates your attitude toward MOOCs? Broken out by the college's full-time student enrollment for all programs and schools.

Enrollment	Destructive and not effective as education	More or less a fad unlikely to have lasting impact	A useful new technology likely to have a significant impact when improved	A useful technology that is having a significant impact right now	A significant advance that will lower costs and improve educational quality
Less than 2,500	0.00%	22.22%	50.00%	11.11%	16.67%
2,500 to 7,499	0.00%	22.22%	55.56%	16.67%	5.56%
7,500 or more	6.67%	13.33%	66.67%	13.33%	0.00%

To what extent do you believe that instruction via MOOCs needs to be supplemented by tutors or other kinds of instructors?

1. This depends on learners' motivation. For access to content alone, instructors may not be required. To replicate a fully online interactive course, the role is significant and required.

2. Under discussion.

3. Early on, extensively supplemental. There needs to be accountability and validation of knowledge/skill. If this can be done, then MOOCs have longevity.

4. To a large extent if we want to make it an effective mode of delivery for instruction at reputable schools.

5. This is higher education, and students should be able to move forward in the courses without tutorial support.

6. To a very large extent.

7. Strongly agree.

8. Tutors may be needed for grading in MOOCs are offered as part of a degree.

9. Minimal.

10. For a majority of students, MOOCs will need supplementation by curated communities - not necessarily tutors or other kinds of instructors.

11. Better if/when supplemented by face-to-face.

12. Very much.

13. I believe that an on-site tutor or liaison is necessary for success in a MOOC.

14. Very much so.

15. Their benefit would be entirely relative to individual student motivation. We, as educators, must recognize that there is a vast wealth of knowledge available. I believe MOOCs add to that knowledge base. My concern is not student access to the knowledge but rather motivation to acquire it and ability to generate individual meaning and learning from it once acquired.

16. A great deal for most students.

17. Yes, this is a must especially for retention purposes and if credit is going to be offered.

18. Completely, though that's mostly outside our institution. Within our institution I don't see MOOCs making sense. We are a residential liberal arts college, an elite college. People come here for a certain reason.

19. Depending upon the nature of the course and the other pedagogies employed in the course.

20. Not much.

21. This is hard to say. It really depends on the audience. For traditional student population, a lot.

22. For modestly qualified, traditional-aged students, MOOCs desperately need to be supplemented. Most of these students are not motivated or disciplined enough to do the work without direct supervision.

23. Depends on level of offering. Lower level may need tutors; graduate level would not.

24. MOOCs are a wonderful extension of the Public Library System. All people should have free access to books as well as course materials. I would not have the same expectation of a book as I would of a 15 week course that teaches, practices and discusses the content or theories contained in a book.

25. Definitively. Research shows that blended learning is the most effective way of delivery in distance education.

26. MOOCs are a good fit for independent learners. Many community college students are not independent learners and would benefit from some kind of supplemental program such as tutors and advisors (to check in and make sure students are on track to learn and to complete).

27. Depends on the course. Intelligent tutoring systems and adaptive learning can provide instructional guidance for some content areas and may or may not need supplemental mentoring. Other areas will need people to help facilitate and guide, especially for novices entering a discipline.

28. Some access to a person is needed, even if only via an on-line chat, email or phone call.

29. MOOCs can be fine at providing adequate instruction. The issue for colleges and universities revolves around awarding of credit for MOOCs in the absence of assessment. MOOCs supplemented with assessment is a more important need.

30. Absolutely!

31. MOOCs are good for general knowledge of random facts or for very technical information. No good for courses where you have to use your mind.

32. MOOCs need peer tutors, instructors and/or discussion groups.

33. Of course supplementation is needed but the cost model for MOOCs here makes that prohibited.

34. Significant student service support will be required.

35. Absolutely critical to raise retention rates (especially for those students wishing to obtain credit).

36. One-on-one online relationships with faculty are essential when taking a MOOC for credit.

37. The completion rate for MOOCs is abysmal. If most college students were independent learners who managed their time well, books alone, much less MOOCs, would be all that was needed for individuals to become competent in content if not in personal skills. The overwhelming majority of students will still need instruction by a well-prepared professional.

38. Extensively to bring the course to life - online is just and extension of the classroom.

39. For traditional undergraduates, supplementing is very important. Graduate and adult will depend on the learner.

40. In most cases for most learners.

Do you believe that MOOCs, either as presently constructed or as rewired in a blended learning setting, constitute an advance in educational effectiveness and/or cost control?

1. This depends on the context. If replacing offerings that currently require high overhead and are targeted for cost reduction, yes. If the intention is to capture enrolments for funding purposes, yes.

2. We believe it might constitute an advance in educational effectiveness.

3. Advancement. They are another form of learning not dissimilar to journal reading, book reading, lab work, or project management.

4. Educational effectiveness yes, cost control not yet.

5. Definitely an advance in educational effectiveness with the proper controls to assure learning.

6. Nope, issues with quality control.

7. Both.

8. Both, they serve to reach people who cannot go to campus and does it at a much lower cost.

9. Not an advance.

10. Both. However, the user authentication process must be improved to insure the person taking the course is the actual person earning the credit.

11. Used in a blended learning setting, MOOCs are both a boost to educational effectiveness and cost control.

12. Yes - helping cost-control/reduction and hence constraining increases in tuition fees & enhancing affordability; also probably improved teaching & learning in some subject areas. Important for both US and English HE where tuition fees are high/increasing. See my 2014 Oxford University Press book, 'Reshaping the University: The Rise of the Regulated Market in Higher Education' (Palfreyman & Tapper).

13. Less success at a reduced cost.

14. Yes.

15. Yes.

16. I see very little benefit in them without restructuring. Teaching requires much more than lecturing. Blending the access to knowledge in a guided process may prove to have academic benefit but for smaller institutions, such as my own, the cost benefit is likely to be minimal...even once the entire field is greatly refined. They certainly do provide a glimpse into a bigger, brighter world...as an educator and lifelong learner; I would always say that is an advantage. I am just not sure how much it advantage it provides to my students today.

17. Greatest impact could be in niche education, greatest profit in large scale, intro courses.

18. Both.

19. I think it may make sense for classes that do not involve either labs or serious writing, when there are exercises that can be computer-graded.

20. Maybe.

21. The bottom line is educational quality and demonstrated student learning. MOOCs could work in a blended learning environment to enhance both educational quality and student learning.

22. Cost control.

23. MOOCs are a disruptive force. As any disruptive inventions, it'll bring a lot of benefits and some unforeseen problems.

24. I have not made up my mind on this question.

25. Verdict still out.

26. College education used to be a state and federal priority and both students and colleges used to receive much more government funding than they do currently. MOOCs do not change the fact that higher education has an enormous impact on one third of all young people. Another third do not need a college education because they are capable of teaching themselves a broad array of material and already think critically and can take a dialectical approach within their community. The final third are not prepared yet to take advantage of college opportunities either because of their poor HS experience or general lack of maturity and will need to apply themselves in this area once they have gained more maturity or preparation.

27. Useful to provide a wider range of options to students.

28. Absolutely. They improve quality and reduce costs, but faculty perceive them as a threat to job security, since we opened this discussion.

29. No.

30. I think MOOCs have the most promise for blended or flipped learning.

31. Yes. See my articles in EDUCAUSE Review Online.

32. Both.

33. The present version of MOOCs are nothing more then chunked sets of content made available for free (or near free) to the masses. This is no great advance in education. It may help contain costs. The advance in education will come when the "massively" part of MOOCS becomes a reality. The integration and commentary of massive numbers of students/users with instructional content will be an advance in education.

34. Not in effectiveness. Yes in terms of cost containment.

35. We limit enrollment in our online courses to ensure quality interaction between the faculty and students. MOOCs don't allow for such close interaction between professor and students. They might help control costs, but possibly at the expense of educational effectiveness.

36. The worse problem with MOOCs is that they give a narrow point of view. Education is about multiple points of views and ways of doing things. MOOCs decrease creativity and make students into followers and not leaders.

37. Yes.

38. MOOCs in their present iteration are neither effective nor cost effective for our population of interest.

39. Cost control or revenue generator.

40. Yes, in educational effectiveness. Too early to tell on cost control.

41. They may help control cost. I don't think that they will contribute to educational effectiveness in a meaningful way or to the education of the whole person. Most disciplines involve far more than content knowledge, which is the most that MOOCs can offer (to a highly motivated, well-organized, self-disciplined few).

42. Yes if the instructional design is well supported by SMEs.

43. Too much depends on the learner to make a blanket statement. As indicated above, traditional undergraduates will still need support if MOOCS are to be educationally effective so not much cheaper to offer. The advanced/mature learner might provide cost control through use of MOOCS.

44. I believe they are a useful tool and an addition to the range of tools available to educators, but not really as tremendously novel an advance as everyone is presenting them to be.

5. Copyright and MOOCs

What measures has the college taken to assure copyright protection for the institution's MOOCs or for taped lectures, classes, or special events sponsored by the college?

1. Existing copyright policy; developing IP policy.

2. You have to be a student to get access to the lectures.

3. Updating faculty and staff handbook.

4. Working on this now.

5. Copyright enforced through limiting access to registered students and using password protection / IP ranges as well for access o the files.

6. None.

7. None.

8. We hold that the lectures are the intellectual property of the instructors. Therefore, the instructor must release the items before they are made available to anyone internal or external to the institution. If, where, and how they choose to release the information will determine the level of protection available to them.

9. None.

10. Exploring all possible developments.

11. We have revised our IP policy accordingly.

12. Trademark and copyright.

13. We currently have insufficient policies on intellectual property and will be developing them.

14. We have developed an institutional policy guaranteeing copyright protection.

15. None.

16. Under review by the General Counsel's Office.

17. Nothing.

18. Our legal office is exploring this.

19. None.

20. We have adopted an intellectual rights policy that addressed this issue.

21. None.

22. We do not keep taped lectures on file.

23. None.

Some MOOCs are from for-profit companies and therefore the fair use provisions of copyright law offer less protection to end users who use copyright materials in their online courses. Has your college taken special measures to assure that instructors in blended learning classes that employ MOOCs do not violate copyright? If so, what are these measures?

1. We have not worked with this issue yet.

2. Problems being identified - once identified, will add to updated F/S Handbook.

3. We are working on this now.

4. Yes, through education and sensitization campaigns with laws in place to punish violators.

5. Do not use MOOC content on online classes other than from Khan Academy. Instructor is responsible for securing copyright.

6. None.

7. Not to date.

8. No.

9. Yes – information.

10. We have not utilized MOOCs or their copyrighted materials at this time.

11. No

12. We need to look into this further.

13. Specialist digital copyright librarian for advice and guidance.

14. Training faculty and students on academic integrity and disseminating the policy.

15. No.

16. Yes. Under the auspices of the Office of Online Programs along with the library system. Instruction on copyright law and best practices re copyright are provided as part of the online course development process.

17. We do not have faculty using MOOCs in their courses at this time.

18. We do not use MOOCs yet because they are a bunch of garbage.

19. Yes, adherence to policy.

20. The issue is addressed in our copyright and intellectual property policies.

21. Yes.

22. Not yet.